# Heavyweight Champion
# of the Night

Wolff Bowden

To Rafael,
May these words
bring you poems as leaves
to the arms of the oak!

— Wolff

for Beauty

## FIRST EDITION

Gratitude is due to the
editors of the following publications where
some of these poems first appeared.

Asheville Poetry Review, "Roofing in Belize"; Daily Constitutional,
"Ages of Magic"; Iconoclast, "The Last Lover" & "Riverside"; Vero
Beach Press Journal, "On the Night Before Bypass"; Urban Stillness,
"The Stone Age"; West Wind Review, "Cellular Vultures"

**OTHER BOOKS BY WOLFF BOWDEN**
Orphanage of Imagination (2002)

WOLFFANTASTIC.COM
THEORPHANTRAINS.COM
GRATITREE.COM

wolffpoet@yahoo.com
wolff@wolffantastic.com

# CONTENTS

# Ghost of a Gecko

I could not bring you roses because
the wind stole their scent. I could not
bring you seashells, there were mollusks
and hermits still in them.

I could not bring you a bouquet of stars;
though I leapt from my roof, they were
still too far. I could not show you the sand
palace I built, the tide came eagerly in.

I could not bring you a gecko, to eat
the mosquitoes that attack your skin.
The gecko was trapped beneath my blanket
and my knee accidentally crushed him.

I was so sad, I built a little ship out of driftwood,
gave him a funeral on last night's ocean.
I had no sail, my love, so I had to use this poem.

The wind carried it away,
along with the scent of your roses,
across the sleeping mollusks in your seashells,
past your demolished sand palace,
where the ghost of the gecko dances,
between walls the sea swept away.

And now, I have only this story,
which I'm certain you'll never believe,
how I ended up here, Love, with nothing
but a few grains of sand on my feet.

# Poetry Reading

When I reach the podium
all I want to be is this poem.
I don't want to be a man standing here
reading this poem. Not even a brilliant man.
Not even a genius. I just want to be
these words in your ears. I want to be sound
plunging down your auditory canal
into the damp expanse of your mind,
over the reef of your brain
where sea turtles and angelfish flap their happy fins,
stirring sand to the surface.
I want to be that sand and that sea
and the words that make it happen.
Because every heart becomes an ocean
the moment it starts to listen.

# However Homeward

When all cities blend into one incessant street.
When pigeons flock so thick a blizzard of popcorn won't
appease the hollow hunger of their beaks.

When the homeless begin begging not for a quarter, fifty cents,
but as one asked yesterday: *can you spare a million?*
I've spent as many words in search of love,
bringing the dictionary to the brink of extinction,
marching my semantic army down alleyways,
where they're choked by memoirs of urine,
ambushed by dumpsters of burning manuscripts.

I have marched them to certain slaughter in the name
of art like this. In your name. In mine. In the names of women
and men, of loneliness, vast and unspoken.

When I have no dance left for street musicians
whose horns blast spittle in the faces of children,
whose guitars hang heavy in their arms like
tombstones wrenched from a graveyard.

I will seek you far from this curb of blood,
where no one holds my hand when I cross the infinite street,
lined with strip clubs and piercing parlors, beckoning with the
cold pink glow of neon. A shopping bag, empty of all but wind,
swirls before my feet like a sheath of tattooed skin.

When I walk these sulfuric sidewalks, jammed with humanity,
and feel nothing, not empathy, not some symbiotic heartbeat,
not even time bleeding out of me as it bleeds out of them, not
even the ache inside the minds of retarded children, whose
gnarled fists make me think they're boxing invisible gods.

Because all gods are invisible now, in this deliquescent country,
where lives melt to sums. Even you are invisible, Love.
Only your shape is outlined in clouds crossing the sky.

Maybe that's why the growling began,
the growling which rose from the part of me that
was never born, will never perish.
Growling which grows louder every hour I'm without you.

Growling deeper than the well where the children in my marrow
pump blood to mix the concrete of my bones.
Growling I have fed with the fiction of distance,
the mythology of movement.
Growling that bids me throw my compass rose into the river
so the giant carp will know from which direction I'll return.

When these mirrored skylines teach me the futility of travel.
When taxis can take me nowhere I haven't been. When my soul
seeks its reflection in a gum-spot on the pavement.

Then and only then, my lips against your stomach
like a violin bow against strings, I'll whisper the critical syllables
that will shape your name from silence.

And in the curve of your neck I will forget how lost I have been,
how nocturnal, how anonymous on the ark of the subway car,
where two by two we climb aboard to avoid
the festering flood. But I step off alone at a stop I do not know
and mount the scabby stairs, pale as a newborn ghost.

Finished with these rivers of people, I
am walking out of the cities, every one, over the water,
across the bridge, the bay, the ocean, all of it. I will
walk across this sentence, holding the planks of
paper together with my ink-stained feet, moving
across this rainy Monday afternoon in search of you.

# Dating in the Animal Kingdom

I know a few trails where we could
grab a bite to eat. Nothing fancy, maybe
a few mice, a weasel if we're lucky.
And after that, we could watch the moon.
The moon is great. Endless entertainment.
I could howl for you. I could howl for you
on a trail I know. You could watch me howl
and you could howl, too, if you're in the mood.
And who knows what might happen after that?
We might scratch our furry backs against a pine-stump
or crunch ferns beneath our paws.
And I won't have to get you home at any particular hour
since we're always home out here
in the green and bristling darkness.
I could climb on top of you, if the moment seems right,
even if the whole forest is watching.
Because we don't understand the word shy.

We could enjoy each other's wildness for a while.

Like I say, nothing fancy,
a trail lined with ferns, a moon, me and you.
And maybe, just maybe,
if we're lucky: puppies.

# Roofing in Belize

After the 67th hurricane this century, we began
at last to understand the missionaries
who told us the good book would save us from the lash
of eternal hellfire, the sour mango taste of poverty.

Even if we had money, there were no shingles in the city.
The Prime Minister glued them over pot-holes
so he could win his re-election. They crumbled
to coffee grounds within a week.

Uncle Myron, the police officer, through his thin window
at the station, watched a single flying shingle
decapitate a looter in one second.

In the eye of the storm we took shelter in
the concrete block church on Hecker Road.
The missionaries had fled for America seven days before,
a timespan they said was enough for God to build a whole
new world. So many iguanas died, we crunched their
bones on our walk home, carrying boxes of Bibles on our
shoulders, singing Creole songs.

What was left of our roof was leaking on the bedsheets
and the babies, so we dunked the Bibles in creosote and
laid them down like shingles.
Our roof looked like the heavens:
pitch black, sparkling here and there.
Two hundred Bibles crucified
by constellations of roofing nails.

# Ghostmaking

You can start anywhere, with anything.
The tap of your fingerprint on an
unsuspecting ant. The release of a rope
tied to a ship suddenly adrift. The ripping
of a weed from dirt and flinging it onto
the roof where it's corpse will shrivel,
whoosh off in the wind. You can stop
calling a friend, without farewell or
explanation. Lean into, then away from
the delicious press of a kiss. Every breath
is one more breath you'll never take again.
Every night with her. Every night with him.
Every moment, you should know this,
is another ghost in the making. Maybe
it's terrifying to think about such things.
Maybe that's why the leaves outside
my window, so brave, so green
are shaking.

# The First Kiss

There's a sheer cliff in Muskoka,
forty or fifty feet, with a waterfall
coming in from the East, filling a
deep pool, ringed by lips of slick granite.

You're up on the highest edge of it,
wanting to flee, your bare feet
gripping the rust-colored gravel,
your heart leaping against your ribs
like a lion against a sliding glass door.

And you feel like your life could end
at any moment. The lion is bashing the
glass so hard you can't understand
why it hasn't shattered, how it is that
you're still here. You look for a rock
to plant the ball of your right foot,
to shove off into the air.

You lean into the wind, your legs flickering
away from the rock. The lion inside is suddenly still.
You are falling, now, pulling your arms
flat against your sides.

When you hit the water, she sucks
you like a tongue, she pulls you inside.
You realize this isn't the end, but
the beginning of your life. She has
horse-kicked the wind from your lungs.
You rise fast, take a deep breath of light.

# LightLand

Welcome to the amusement park of Life.
We only have one ride, for which you will
pay a single, startling price. But you pay
on your way out, not your way in. We begin
by strapping you into a suit of bones and
muscle and skin. We paint your eyes the
perfect color to see the blue plumbago
blooms of morning, the perfect pink of
lips. We give you hinged fingers to
soar from tree to tree, gripping the
bouncing branches. We give you fingertips
to stroke the warm and hungry skin of
your beloved, before reaching for a guitar
and pressing the strings to make the
air in dim rooms tremble. We give you
a voice and language so you can easily
make friends. You are the carnival ride.
You are light pouring out of a box-car
heading West on a moonless Thursday night.
You will love this. You will cry.
You will shudder in the vise of time.
Unwrap your senses. Taste the world.
Open your eyes. Stay alive. Ride.

# The L Word

Here's the most interesting thing:
I'm the son of a lesbian. Which may make you wonder
how I got here to begin with. How I grew into this
stunning sheath of bones writing this poem.
How I came to have these starfish hands
that can crawl under the seas of your dreams.
Well, here's the truth of it: Love put me on this planet.
Love made my father wander in my mother's wilderness.
Love made them dance in the darkness. Love wrote
the speech of me, and I landed, dripping with
life, at the center of this podium. My father shouted
*I have a son!* My mother rubbed my feet.
I asked them for a brother and Love helped them
build one for me. But now, I'm peering into other facets
of this diamond of existence. I need to lift my pen and
focus. To look the thing square in the face, to stare at the
unflinching orchids: I'm the son a lesbian.
Some people can't understand how something like this
happens. How two souls can blend breath and secrets
without a single penis. How breasts can
press breasts and light can bind feminine skin.
Well, the truth is, Love doesn't care where
it lives. It can live in two women's bodies.
In the bodies of bluebirds and pines. In my
father and my mother. In a shoebox on
an empty shelf in an abandoned apartment.
And we must keep Love safe, no matter where it appears.
Because hearts can only beat our blood
from way out there, to right in here.

# Lullaby to Light

It is not the suit of skin. It is the fire within.

Though your suit might have faithful muscles
in all the right places, moving when you think them to,
pulsing with blood and purpose.

Though your spine might ask the right questions
of the night.

It is not your breasts or your lips or the
warm butterfly between your thighs.

It is the fire. Always, the fire.

It is not even the room where I made love to you.
It is our breath, braided, hidden from the winds of late
afternoon.

It is not the planets of your pupils. It is the fire under the
shimmering sea of your irises.

Remember, it is not the suit of skin.
It is the light of the fire within.

It is not the skin of ink, but the blaze inside the pen.
Not these thin lines of ants marching into
the blizzard of an empty page.
It is the light of language in the fire of their silence
that keeps them warm and brave.

# February Wedding

These are the vows the sea makes to the beach
wave after wave, day after day, and even
on into the night, with families of stars
standing witness.

This is the first kiss, replayed for an audience
so all eyes will know where you're going,
where you've been.

By watching two rivers become one ocean.
By seeing for themselves how blue and yellow
really do make green, the color God gave leaves
to pull love straight from the sun.

The rain says *I do* to the roots
and the surf roars *I do* to the shore.
Your hearts unfold their small, muscular, arms
and stand there, hugging, in the dark.

Because this is the point where the rest of us vanish,
the moons of mothers, the fires of fathers, the
torches and flowers of cousins and friends.

And you are no longer you, but every couple
who ever loved, every couple who ever will.
his heart drumming her blood
her heart drumming his.

# Three Seasons

This is the Preparation.
The canvas being stretched like a sheet of light in your
hands. Bright staples popping out of the gun, your forearm
sore from flexing. This is where the circular saw
gets sharpened before spinning into clean sheets of wood.
Where basil is plucked, one leaf at a time, for the evening's
sesame stir-fry. This is the letter you write to make her fall
in love with you, the song you sing to summon strength.
This is pigment smeared on canvas in ways
you cannot explain. This is the storm-cloud hovering like a
black slug over the house, lugging its lifetime of rain. The
net being tugged through the tides of the author's mind
to catch these words to fill this page.

This is the Incubation.
The work has left your hands. The painting is hanging
eye-level on the gallery wall. There is nothing you have to
do now. Just sit back and watch the warm rain fall. The
rice is sealed beneath the lid of shimmering steel.
The letter is in the mailbox, affixed with exact postage.
The diver has broken the turquoise mirror of the pool
and the judges are whispering among themselves.
You did all that you could. You did your best.
Now it is time for the invisible hands of the universe to
do the rest. You've told her that you love her and now you
need to stare at the stars again. Think clumps of cookie
dough at the center of an oven. Think baby alligators
coiled and growing armor in their eggs. The seeds you
planted yesterday are unpacking their leafy suitcases under
the soil your bare hands spread.

And this is the Illumination.
The spark we wait lifetimes to find. The bedsheets tossed
back, the tiny notebook, the wild scribbling of a pen.
The high-heeled daughter of an oil-baron signing a check
to buy your painting. The first mouthful of the feast
sending a shiver of flavor up your spine. This is Buddha
bowing to the clouds after seven years of silence. The
telephone ringing with the news that your novel will soon
be published. The coelacanth, long-considered extinct,
discovered off the coast of Madagascar.
The light-bulb flashing bright in the cave behind your eyes.
The dream in which you suddenly realize you are
dreaming. The dream in which
you find out you can fly.

# The Beginnings of Religion

Jesus and Mohammed were sitting
one afternoon on the banks of the Nile.
Jesus said, "Mohammed, we should
love them all." And Mohammed smiled.

# Bloodstream

They say you've never seen traffic
until you've been to New Delhi
and churned for five or six hours
in a cauldron of rickshaws and exhaust
of big-horned buffalo and honking
box-trucks, their bumpers painted
with grinning, red demons to keep evil away.
Until you've tasted the grit from the whirling
tire of a bus older than you are.
Until you've dodged a thousand motorbikes
surging like minnows through the river of a red light.
Until you've ridden in a taxi, or on the bumpy
shoulders of a cycle-rickshaw, your driver's
sweaty calves pumping the pedals to earn
his fare of eighty cents. Until you've heard
the symphony of horns and seen the grace
of the drivers in this sector of hell.
They cut each other off constantly,
but you will never hear them yell.
They forgive with a breath.
They are cells in a vein in your leg, pushing on
through their own living dark, moving
North towards the drum that gives them
life, moving home to your own silent heart.

# The Dead That Do Not Know

At the bottom of the Atlantic
there are soldiers running home.
They are leaving a trail of bullets
like copper whelks on the ocean floor.

They can no longer feel pressure or
anger or cold. Yesterday, something
happened, some burst of blood and bone.
But it's like a dream they can't remember
in the blue ocean of morning.
All they know is how to get home.

How to put one word in front of another
in a letter never sent, saying we
are coming home, watch for us
earlier than expected, while gruesome fish
who have learned over millions of years
to make their own luminescence,
keep flickering on and off, like vigil lights,
as the ghosts run through them.

# Constellations of a Face

When he was smaller, I taught him Ursa Minor,
the little bear whose bones were built of stars.
I grabbed his waist in my hands and lifted him high,
almost into the night.

He grinned at the sparkling belt of Orion,
a luminous line above the horizon, and
when I showed him the big bull Taurus
he shook his head. He didn't believe it.
He made me show him again and again
all through the year he was seven.

At nine, he wandered without me, practicing
constellations: Leo, Virgo, Libra.
He patrolled the yard with a notebook,
at midnight, stars dripping from his pen.

Last week, I heard him sobbing
behind the bathroom door, cursing the same skin
I had cursed when I was fifteen.
From forehead to chin, it looked as if
he'd been stung by a herd of scorpions.

Tonight, once again, I lead my troubled son outside
setting his face beside the face of the pock-marked sky.
So he might assess himself again
in the mirror of the heavens.
So his sadness might be lifted into light.

# The Last Lover

Death gets one night with every woman, luring her
into his foggy bedroom with the most final of embraces,
kissing her body back into the blackness between stars.

By then, he's dark with longing.
He has waited all her life, even if Katie's a mere sixteen,
dead behind the wheel of a Mustang.
With accidents like hers, you wonder
if Death was playing fair; did
he throw that raccoon in the road
or hand her that extra beer?

And what about Amy, who drowned in the lake?
Did Death see her, skinnydipping, and
yank her ankles down?

Death has always been greedy, but who can stop him,
what can they say? Where do you think we got the
phrase *drop dead gorgeous* anyway?

Still, I wonder if he's tender, as I am with you tonight,
closing the thick linen curtains against Death's
omniscient eyes. Why do you think I hide you in
the movies, the theater?
Because Death sees through the eyes of insects
and few insects gather there.

Why do you think, when we're walking
through the park on a sunny day,
I tremble at the sight of butterflies
circling your face?

# Run

Just before dawn, on an Indian highway lined with palms,
a four-year-old boy begins a forty mile run.

Five thousand people stand on the mud-crusted shoulders
of the road, draping him with garlands of frangipani
blossoms.

For the first mile, he repeats a prayer to Ganesh.
The second mile brings the memory of
his mother dressing him: his favorite red shorts,
his t-shirt with the emblem of the local police force.

By mile three, he is thinking about the way his coach
laced up his shoes, while humming a Hanuman tune.
Mile four and his legs begin to sweat,
the way they did the day his mother
asked their neighbor if she wanted to buy him.

On that day, he ran across the corrugated wasteland.
Ran through the sharp reeds, the broken bottles by the
gangrene stream, past Jagannath Temple, to the
private sports ground, the white men's track.

Mile six and he is on that track, his coach, who
was just a stranger then, ordering him to run laps
as punishment for trespassing. So he did. So here he is.
Coach came back five hours later and he was still running.

Mile ten and he sees his dead father's face in
the crowd, a smile of jagged teeth, a lift of his
massive black eyebrows. *I am running to*

*Bhubaneswar*, Budhia mumbles, as if the ghost
can hear him.

When he sees the British reporter at mile twenty-one
he nods, peels his lips back for a grin
and whispers, in English, *I am run.*

And as his tiny feet grow still
at the end of the fortieth mile
he knows that his past cannot catch him
as dust circles the worlds of his eyes.

# Night Raft

We are three hundred pounds
of bone and blood and beauty
in a moss-green hammock on a Saturday night.
Most of that beauty is yours and
most of the weight is mine. The
overhead oak-leaves are a star-screen
through which we glimpse those
ancient, faithful sparks.
And we think we're drifting in the wind,
but we're anchored, heart in heart.

# Chinese Zodiac

You sit down to order a simple plate
of chicken chow mein and discover
you're a monkey or a tiger or a snake.

As you munch fried noodles your
paper placemat gives it to you straight:
you are talented and affectionate, marry a sheep.

The goldfish in the tank across the room swim in and out
of a submerged pagoda while you try to remember the
birthdays of every woman you ever loved.
Maybe none were sheep; that's why things didn't work out.

Pouring yourself a tiny cup of tea, barely a mouthful, a
giant's tear, you examine the menagerie on your placemat,
twelve animals printed in red.

Why is a cock compatible with a snake? Why
should a dragon avoid a dog? Perhaps true wisdom lurks
beyond the cliffs of comprehension.

Which is why you lean back into the
vinyl booth and lose interest in the whole idea.
Sure, life is a zoo, people are animals, rats and dogs,
but for now your hunger takes over
as the waiter scoops steaming rice onto your plate.

You eat like a tiger, aggressive and courageous,
wondering if the solitary woman across the room
might be showing signs of timidity, elegance. If so,
she could be a sheep, you two just might make it.

You'll marry in the spring and she'll
give birth to three strong children: Tom,
the tiger, Alex, the rabbit, and Annabell,
the pint-sized dragon.

## Sunrise, South India

This morning, I woke golden
as an acre of wheat, seeded with
the stray flowers of dreams, the orange
of carnations, blue mountains, lost streets.
The sun came up on my face.

Outside my fifth floor hotel room,
forty feet down and three blocks northeast,
a young girl is waking up on a rooftop
rolling up her bedsheet, shaking it a little
to scare out the fleas, the inexorable dust
and whatever small stars
might be left, from the worlds of night,
for the rest of us.

# Night Snails

A man who has never spoken, who never speaks,
lies down to sleep. It is as if the man is an actor
on a ten o'clock sitcom and the room is a
television, locked on MUTE. The sheets don't
even whisper as he pulls them up to his chin.

In seven minutes, his mouth drops open
and a thousand snails stream out,
sewing glistening seams on his pillowcase,
shimmering calligraphy across the sliding glass door
as they flee his room by moonlight.

The snails slide down the street like a band of drunkards,
roaring obscenities, waking the neighbors,
who curse, throw open their windows and
stare, dumbfounded, at the empty air above the snails.

The snails laugh at the stars and howl when
restless dogs bark like gunshots.
They pause in Arlington Park to cheer for the
late-night tennis champions.

By sunrise, they return home,
somewhat muffled, inexpressibly tired,
stacking themselves in the mute man's vocal chords
like a tiny brick wall of silence.

# On the Night Before Bypass

We are the children he made,
huddled around his hospital bed
in the sanitized shadows. The air
in his room is so cold that our
jackets barely subdue the shivers
that climb our spines.
Tomorrow, they will take him away,
saw him in half like a carnival act
and re-direct the river of his blood
in three new aqueducts, hewn from
the flesh of his calves. But for now,
he is laughing, because last night
at two in the morning, a man flung
open the door to his room. My father
sat up and flinched back, lifted his
hands. The man said, *I'm not going
to hurt you, I can promise you that.
I'm here to re-fill the water in the
pitcher beside your bed.* The story
is enough to make all of us laugh,
because the world we live in
is ridiculous, but like fish in a
box of glass or heart-sick men in
small rooms, we're all waiting for
and afraid of change. Our lives
are rarely still.

Blood empties from
our beautiful hearts
and seconds later
is refilled.

# Poetry Reading at Auschwitz

At the end of a day when a dozen among us
died of typhus, refusing to eat anything, even
sunlight, even snow, he lines us up as
if he's going to read another list of numbers
of who will go to the gas chambers and who,
back to breaking stone. But this time,
he isn't reading numbers or regulations
or pointing at the umber ceiling beam
and threatening to hang the next man who
speaks. No, this time, he's pacing on the
urine-soaked straw of our bunk-room,
hesitantly reading a love poem. *Gretchen,*
he reads, *taught me a lesson. Her breasts
were like hills, they gave me thrills.*
I bite my lip to keep from laughing, drawing
blood which I swallow hard. When his
poem is finished, I think of my own,
written in the scars on my arms, the black
flap of crows in the sky, dedicated to my
missing, I pray she's still living, wife.
Then I pull one heavy hand off of each
toothpick thigh, and force them to bang
together using all my withering might.
I clap as hard as I can. I nod. I smile.
Two men at the back who do not clap
will soon swing from the beam over
my head. That, in itself, is a poem. If
I had a pen, I would write it on
the paper-thin tatters of my pants:
the leaves in the work yard are dead
but still they lift their hands, they dance.

# Creation of the Cats

It happens in tiny sweat-shops
in every loop of this ball of yarn
we call our world, young girls, no older
than five or six, slipping away after dinner,
explaining that they must prepare
a tea-party for their dolls.

Then, sitting down in secret,
with needles as long as their fingers,
these little artisans begin
sewing soft fur to whiskers
and attaching, as if by magic,
the precious paws.

You can sometimes hear them through closed doors
whispering kittens into existence.

Or whistling the full range of bird songs
so the kittens will know how to hunt them
when they're born.

And if you hear a fluttering sound, don't be alarmed.
She's just making sure the throat motor purrs properly.

In a little while, she'll pop in two amber eyes
and twist the ears upright. She'll purse her lips
as if for a kiss
and breathe the beast to life.

# The Summoning

Ask it to come. Ask it to stay.
Ask it to cast rose petals across
the calm of your sleeping face.
Make a home for it in the curve
along the upper lip of your beloved,
so that when you kiss her,
you will never forget its taste.
Let it dance with your fingers
on the stage of her shoulderblades.
Let it hover like a hummingbird
in the dark carnation of her heart,
its beak like a needle of light,
its wings scattering green sparks.
And until she welcomes you there,
let it hide between her thighs.
Then, let it rise with your pulse
through her spine. Let its invisible
hands touch down on every cell
in your body, every tiny drum.
Ask it to stay. Ask it at once.
Pray if you must. Ask it to come.

# Highway Under Heaven

This time, while you are away
I become intimate with the distance to outer space
stepping outside, into the crisp wind of a
January night, inspecting constellations
for new additions, seeing if the Pleiades are now
eight sisters instead of seven, checking the moon
for the imprint your breasts would make
if you slept in that bed of ashes.

Back here, on Earth, a huge wave toppled
a lighthouse in Madagascar. A meteor fell
straight down, towards the house, and burned
out seconds from the shingles. I drove the
long road to meet you in silence
as if floating on a liferaft
in the artery of a sleeping child.

I imagined all the others, like myself, moving, tonight,
towards the ones they love. A father
driving his eighteen wheeler home to his daughters
and wife. A mother slipping into the rooms
of her sleeping sons after a twelve hour
surgical shift at the hospital. Love coming back
to the planet after slipping away, for a time,
to labor in the company of stars. And out
among these arriving lights, you:
a smile with arms.

# Far from the Swamp

When a frog checks into a hotel,
I'd imagine he doesn't express a preference
about the size of his bed. King or two Queens,
it's all the same to Mr. Green. He doesn't even
give a damn about the thread-count of the sheets.

And forget the key-card, he can squeeze beneath
the heavy, dark-red door. With a flick of his
tongue, the lights snap on in the room.
The carpet is somewhat damp and sticky.
This pleases him immensely.

Watching a bit of televised war coverage,
a bit of blood spilled in Iraq, he wonders
when people will get tired of killing
and re-discover the joy of swimming.

Opening the window to night, he watches
his dinner fly in: three gnats, two houseflies,
a bevy of bumbling mosquitoes.
With his belly full, he croaks for a while,
hoping to find a wife, but an agitated fist
thumping the wall is his only reply.

So, silently, he makes his way towards
the only space in the room that matters,
the only space that can help his homesickness,
the only space he can really rest:
in the pale, smooth pond of porcelain,
he splashes down, for the night,
in the toilet.

# A Brief History of Sweet

If you write the word honey
on a bright white page and lick it,
will you taste the sweetness of
a thousand paper bees? Or, if
you fall in love with a girl who
works in a sugar factory, will her
skin take your tongue dancing
over dunes of crystal sweet?
Maybe sweetness has nothing to
do with the story of the tongue
and everything to do with love,
so that even if she quit her job
at the factory and sat singing on
the street, you could kiss her
guitar-hardened fingertips and
taste the wind-swept sugar canes
of the Dominican Republic
where a group of small, dark
children, given a single soda
as a tourist's gift, are passing
it around from mouth to mouth
from sip to shining sip.

# All the King's Light

Today, like other days, the sun still finds your face.
But tomorrow, like all tomorrows, your private star,
maybe all the stars, could be swallowed
by some giant tadpole of blackness
in the puddle of space.

Today, it's yours; tomorrow, who knows?
Your car with its fragrant leather. Your house
with its smiling door. Your watch with its steady hands
and tiny quartz shard for a heart. Your style.
Your clothes. Even your laughing father,
whose face is a foggy mirror of your own.

And his silver mane reminds you that death is
on his way, that you need to accept change
as wood accepts flame. That even the beautiful body
beside you in bed this morning
will get up and walk away.

Everything follows this law
but it still takes you by surprise
when your dog disappears
or your cat is gone overnight.

So you walk from room to room,
taking inventory of your life, the red sweater
on your dresser, the smiling picture of your wife,
making sure nothing else has vanished
even with tears in your eyes.

# Last Minute Valentinos

As I wander the drug store aisles
in search of a humidifier to soften
the dry, February nights, I weave
through the flustered faces of
three small men, picking up boxes
of chocolate, putting them down again,
mumbling to each other in Spanish.

Their pants are dusted with leaves
and their shirts are torn in ways that make
you think of branches.

I should probably mention that it's
almost evening, that the aisle is almost
completely red with splashes of
glowing white, that I cannot leave until
I see what these bronze-skinned
soldiers of citrus bring home to their
expectant wives, who are probably gathered
together at this moment, at work in the
same kitchen, frying beef flautas and
mashing avocado and laughing at their men.
As if they already know Ramon is clutching
two fluffy bears in his fist and Juan is
struggling to decipher the English
hieroglyphics on a chocolate box
and Pablo, clueless Pablo,
is buying Maria
a ridiculous dog.

# Ages of Magic

When I was five
I thought the space-bar on the keyboard
was the button you pushed
to launch another space shuttle into the sky.
And at six, I was sure the flea market
was where you went to buy a tiny circus.
At seven, I told strangers
that the end of the world was clasped
securely in my closed fist.
I died mysteriously on the day I turned eight,
but was resurrected the next morning
by a prayer my mother made
with a stack of pancakes.
By nine, I was already a giant.
Every step I sloshed into the swamp
made herons and raccoons flee
and instead of frogs I would find
green lions on lilly pads
fast asleep.

And now that I'm a man
and mysteries have been carved down to facts
I still stand, sometimes, in the Ocean of Night
catching fish of wild ink
in these paper nets.

# Heavyweight Champion of the Night

This is the weight of 2 St. Bernards.
This is the weight of 20 Abyssinian cats.
This is the weight of a barrel of Argon gas.

Remember this weight. Remember this naked chest against
your naked chest. This is the exact weight of something
words fumble to express.

This is the weight of the laughter of ten thousand children.
This is the weight of the sun's face wearing the moon as a
mask. This is the weight of wishes, half-risen in a light rain.
This is the weight of again and again and again.

Remember this chest. Remember this breath.
This is the weight of all I am and all I have.
This is the weight of language lost in a forest of silence.
This is the weight of friendship
dressed in fire's bright rags.

Remember this weight, this night, this space.
This is the weight of all I can't say.
This is the weight of my ribs on your ribs, two cages
pressed so close, the songbirds inside can kiss.

This is the weight of two small, pale objects
dropped from a tower, from Newton's fists,
falling at the same sweet speed
in the gravity of happiness.

# Mataam Fez

I stole a little girl's soul in Morocco,
kidnapped her essence in a photograph,
and when I was finished, as a consolation,
I gave her a ball-point pen.

On nights like this, I wonder what she's doing with it.
I wonder if she might be writing herself a new soul,
To replace the one I stole so long ago.
I wonder if it's possible to write a new soul,
then answer my own question with the
fact that I'm sitting here.

Isn't that exactly how life hits? We're emptied, suddenly,
without warning, by a stranger or a lover, an accident or
intention, and we sit at a table, begging our soul back
from the other side of the desert.

On nights like this I turn on every light in
my small room because I feel the Moroccan girl
growing, grown already: with every passing hour,
shadows cast their nets over her, draping her destiny
in ways she never imagined, binding her body
to a man she first kisses after he owns her.

He'll never suspect he doesn't own
her completely, that he's not the only man
removing her veil in the dark.
He'll never know her soul hides in America, with me,
free as the morning I stole it, basking in the glare
of the light on my desk.

Though her body may be shadow-bound,
her soul swims bright in this ink.
And every night she sits on the toilet to write, the
only place he won't follow, I'll sit in a different solitude,
yet, all the same, beside her.

On nights like this, I wish I had given her a box of
matches, not a pen, so that instead of her ink pulsing
through my wrists, I could feel it every time she tried
to ignite this emptiness.

I would feel it as flames ate her veil
and know the moment had come to return what I stole,
to throw open the doors of her childhood with
these simple hands of language,
letting out the woman, letting in the wind,
so that her fire would rise with conviction
as she struck the last match
to burn him.

# Building the Perfect Bear

In Rwanda there are twelve-year-olds
hacking each other's hearts
out of their chests with machetes,
but here in America, at the Sunrise
Strip Mall, we are building our own
bears, choosing little blue-jeans for
their stuffed and stubby legs, picking
out just the right boots to hike across
our plush carpets. Over in Iraq, kids
are learning to crawl without legs
since our troops firebombed their mud huts
while hunting the Taliban, which makes
perfect sense to us as we choose hats
for our cute little bears. No matter that
the Taliban is based in Afghanistan.
We're glad to be destroying Iraq as long
as we don't have to go there, as long
as we can sit in air-conditioning, sipping
lattes, building bears. If women in Africa
are getting their genitals cut off as a
rite of passage, we won't dwell on that.
We have more to attend to here,
such as, what our bear's name should be,
what color shirt he should wear.

# The Legend of Sleepy Hollow

Sometimes, I get tired of being a poem.
Sometimes, I get tired, and
I want to be a racehorse that has never lost,
galloping across a field of ice,
my hooves scarring the tundra,
my coal-black nostrils blowing steam
into the dreams of sleeping women.

Sometimes I get tired of being these words.
I want to retreat into ordinary things.
To slip into the mushrooms
on the plate of chicken marsala you're eating.
To slip down your throat into darkness.
To return to the world
as a puff of breath from your lungs.

Sometimes I get tired of this paper and
this ink. I would rather have 206 bones
and a tongue and a pale set of teeth.
Lips and muscles painted with a generous
coating of skin. So I could slip into
bed beside you, as you dream of
a stallion leaving hoof-prints on
a frozen field: black marks on a
white sheet, a completely
unchosen poetry, a poetry
made for a world of light and speed

a world where everyone loves fire
and no one ever reads.

# Garage Sailing

We set out as early as we can.
Coffee on our breath. A newspaper
clutched like a map in my grandfather's hands.

Yesterday, these were streets, but on this misty, March
morning, they are inlets, intercoastal channels
deep enough to accommodate
the long slope of our keel.

The passenger seat is a crow's nest
where I scan the horizon for signs.

Sometimes, on a concrete beach,
we find a shipwreck: unstrung guitars,
battered books, candles kissed twice by fire
and then abandoned, set adrift. Tools
too tired to turn another bolt
in their owner's fist.

This is how we buy the flotsam of another's life:
the mirrors that have seen them naked, the
half-spent sorcery of spices, the old trunks
that once held the sweaters of daughters grown and gone.

The wind shifts our sails and we're off.
To another driveway, another lonely dot
on this archipelago of the lost,
in search of the pirate who has forgotten that
his treasure is buried here
between the things we hold onto,
the things that disappear.

# Ocean Season

If winter ever gets so wicked
that the comforting adjectives freeze
and the only descriptives left are cold and frozen,
you can always walk down to the beach inside me.

Where the water is blue as blood before air hits
and seagulls carry golden bundles of sunlight on their
wings. The sand is an endless sacrifice. So many shellfish
gave their lives to bring this softness to your feet.

So abandon your coffee beside the snow-choked window.
Throw your clothes in the corner to give the spiders
caverns in which to weave
tiny maps of web that lead
to the beach inside me.

Where you alone are welcome
along the warm curves of my ribs.
Where waves pound the shore with my pulse.
Where the wind is a constant friend.
Where clouds are vaporous iguanas
lounging out near the horizon, soaking up sun
perfect reminders of how to do nothing
in case you've forgotten how it's done.

# Riverside

A rat and a man sit eating bread by the river.
The man looks at the rat. The rat looks at the man.
The river rushes past, going where all rivers go,
making no progress, because if the whole river reaches
its destination, it's dead.
The rat feels sorry for the river, because the river never
rests. It's constantly taking snapshots of the sky. The man
is glad he isn't the rat, though he's not exactly sure why.

The man has a sudden urge to kick the rat, but instead he
throws it a piece of bread. *Life doesn't choose what form it's
born into, and it must be really tough to make it as a rat.*

The river wonders how far it will have to flow before the
man and the rat appear to be roughly the same size, the
same thing, small packages of blood and hunger wrapped
in hairy skin. Soon, the river says, *here, I can no longer
tell the difference,* and the poet is forced to ask: "which of
you is the rat and which the man?"

It is a trick question because nothing will be confirmed
no matter who raises his hand. By now, each is a little bit
of the other, anyway. The man has imagined himself a rat.
The rat has imagined himself a man.

By now they are close enough to sit by the same river,
breathing the same air, eating the same bread, and waiting,
though neither acknowledges it, for the same impending
darkness, in which men and rats and carp churn the same
water, swimming and swimming and swimming,
but never really returning, to here, or even there.

# Brothers of the Lake

*for Zach*

You are the closest thing to me
the world will ever see.
When you laugh, the sky gets a look at my teeth.
When you cry, the seas of my sadness increase.
I wonder how many nights of our lives
we have dreamt the same dreams.

Because we both grew in the same warm room
listening to the mantra of our mother's heartbeat,
listening through her dome of light for the sounds
of falling leaves, the whispers of folding laundry,
the songs of pianos and language.

We are shrapnel from the same sweet explosion,
confetti from the same New Year's Eve.
Our veins are roads on matching maps
of the same undaunted country.

Brother, you are my mirror, the unbroken surface
of the lake we grew up with, the lake of our childhood
with its alligator scars on otherwise flawless black skin.
The lake where you went fishing without me
on early foggy mornings.

I want you to know I was with you, even then.
To know when you watched a swirling fish
my eyes, also, followed him.

# The Window in My Father

Tomorrow, they will crack
my father open like a pistachio
in its suntanned shell. He will be
sleeping, the saw will descend,
they will sew a new song into him.
Three new rivers will run through
the surgeon's fingers and they will
set a new course in the gravel
of impending years.

And his surgical team
will see what he has never seen:
his own heart, the muscle that
clenched like thunder in his chest
as I was conceived, the sculpted
clay of Georgia fields, the drum
of rage and tenderness, the conch under
deep waters, crawling towards
the sun

searching for love, in oceans of rust
even as they sew him up.

# Quantum Physics

They say science was forever changed
when they realized one object could occupy
two places at the same time,
but some of us already knew this.

The unshaven fisherman and
the smooth-skulled monk capturing
the same sunset in four separate eyes.

An alpine lake and the ocean both wearing
the same damp robe of constellations.

Or even this poem, being read by a
red-haired physicist in her California lab
while at exactly the same moment
beside a campfire in rural Vermont
flames are illuminating this page,
backpacking this poem down a trail
into a lone man's mind
so that suddenly, our physicist
isn't just simply in her lab
listening to Mozart, cleaning pipettes,
but is also swimming in the neurons
of a man she's never met.

# Cellular Vultures

Driving on highway 50, I see a hundred vultures
on a cell phone tower, listening to our conversations,
tuning in with their feathers. Hearing Mark tell Tom to
meet him at O'Reilly's Pub at 8 o'clock, hearing Marlene
complain about her dwindling daytime minutes,
her outrageous roaming charges.

Buzzards are, by nature, somewhat lazy. Circling and
searching for dead things, they're really only piggy-backing
the wind. But now, it's even easier: they merely sit and
listen.

The cell tower vultures look bored, with good reason:
George is describing, play by play, the entire football
season. Joey, at Millennium Mall, is shouting *What up?* to
Kim. *Just chillin'*, Kim mumbles back, shifting the phone to
her other ear.

Then, a woman named Clara is calling everybody,
one after another, telling the neighborhood about
Timmy Donovan, who drowned in his flooded cellar.
Hearing this, the vultures begin to flap their wings.
A fresh one! A feast in the making!

One lone vulture flies away. He searches for a phone
booth, rare in this day and age, and finds one outside a
small-town supermarket. Opening the attached phone
book, he lets his ponderous claws do the walking. He flips
through white pages, trying to link a place to the name
of a boy he's never met,
a boy whose minutes ran out today.

# Song of Soap

He waits for you in the shower,
waits for your body, for the sweat
on your breasts, the sand on your ankles,
the stains this afternoon's rain left on your neck.

You step into the steady spray and casually reach for him,
your hands impelled by habit, his lather growing
smooth between your fingers once again.

All your life, all your half-blind mornings and collapsing
nights, he's been there, dissolving himself to remove
the smears the world left on you.

And tonight, for some reason, you realize you've taken him
for granted, like a lover you touch but never talk to,
a friend you've forgotten who sends you a painting of
your own face, one cold Christmas.

You apologize out loud, feeling silly, spreading him
on your hips, between your legs, behind your ears,
wondering what you can possibly do to make it up to him.

Before you rinse him away, into the sewer's gurgling grave,
you rub him on your cheeks and promise to ask your
friend the poet to write a few lines for him.

So that each person who reads these words
will bless the shower's humble saint,
so that no soul who reads this poem
will ever see soap
the same.

# Alligator Solo

In the swamp behind my brother's house
rests a baby alligator skull. On a sheet of drying mud,
a white muzzle of bone.

When the wind blows through his eyes
his mouth makes a drawn-out sigh
as if he's surrendered at last to the birth of his ghost,
to the inevitable rhythm of rain
washing away his bones.

If nothing else, he can whisper a song about no longer
having to eat; he can sing the freedom of
charging through the swamp without leather skin or teeth.
He can sing the song about no one fearing him anymore,
no man hacking him apart with a hatchet
seventeen Saturdays ago.

He can sing a song for twilight, just now coming on.
For the white face of the moon, the hurricane of stars.
Or he can sing a long, haunting solo for the oak leaves,
his vast, green audience, his gentle friends,
who, at this very moment,
are already clapping for him.

# Inscription

In this book is written
something from a man to a woman.
Not in chapter one or any chapter thereafter
but on the first page, in the white space.
Before the story even begins, he confesses
that she is the mahogany ancient shamans carved
into goddesses and gods. She is the first gulp
of sea swallowed by a newborn whale. She
is the reason he rushes home each night from
his job, where he installs windows and doors.
Because, in her presence, he is a tiny astronaut
weightless on the moon,
awestruck by one spectacular star.
Beside her, he is a ship, his sail billowing with
every wind that ever blew men home.
Tonight, as I hold you in the dark,
as we curl together, like one small victory of peace
in life's fast, unceasing war
I wonder if they're curled up, too, somewhere
like this, the way we are.

# Children of the Mind

Thoughts are unplanned children,
born running, from the heat of some moment
in which heartbreak or worry spawned them,
into the black bedroom behind your forehead.

Thoughts don't knock, though you've
told them a thousand times.
They clamber onto your freshly
washed sheets, shouting, dropping clods of
soil, with firefly blood smeared on
their cheeks so you can see them.

They don't belong here, in your silence.

These children were grown long ago,
so you tell them it's time to leave,
to go to college, get jobs, get married,
whatever it is thoughts do when they
leave the thinker's nest.

*Sure, sure,* they say, but then slink
into the kitchen to bang the pans and pots.
To eat your Rocky Road ice-cream
straight from the tub.

Then thoughts borrow your Porsche without asking,
drive to the seedy nightclub by the beach,
and return at dawn, arm in arm with emotions.

They crash into your room again,
bringing their new friends. Suddenly
you're in bed with fear, rage, anxiety,
sorrow, despair. *Make room*, thoughts say,
but instead you make paper.

Clean, white sheets of paper, smooth
as a blind man's just-shaved cheek.

For every thought, you use a
a fresh sheet. You write them out,
you pin them down in ink.

And while you're at it,
you write down the emotion each
thought brought home, then you tuck
each piece of paper in an envelope
and address it to Saudi Arabia, Kyoto, Madagascar,
the farthest places you can think of,
places where your thoughts might grow up and become
winds of wild laughter
in a quiet Chinaman's lungs.

# Dear God

I am writing to let you know
we've drawn lines on all the oceans.
Oh, and I'm sorry to tell you this, but we've been
slaughtering each other over details again.
Your appearance, for instance.
Or, the things you may
have said two thousand years ago.
Most of us believe you have a penis,
that your chest is solid as stone.
Though a few have imagined the truth:
that you're more of a woman with a man
deep inside her, ejaculating stars. Only, there's
no separation between you, no he and she,
no double flame. You are soil woven into
root and cloud married to sky.
Even the moon couldn't sift the darkness
from your infinite night. I'm writing to tell you
we love you, though we cannot agree on your name.
And we're still pretty much
as you made us, our faces like flowers
in a wild bouquet.

# Anatomy of a Poet

In case you haven't noticed
the poet's fingers are eight pens
and his thumbs are pink erasers
though he rarely uses them.
His nose is a magnet for marvels:
a robin's nest outside a dental office
woven from a single mint strand of floss,
a snow-shoe on a Florida beach,
the Spanish songs of conquistadors
you mumble in your sleep.
His breath, by the way, is ink.
And he never gets tired; he could wander
in the forest of metaphor for 1000 miles.
Sometimes, he writes a love poem
and publishes it in his smile.
But let me tell you his secret,
an observation you may have missed:
His lips are paper
awaiting a kiss
from one like you
on a night like this.

# The First Painting

I always imagine him hungry on a stone cold January
morning, at the lip of a cave in what today would be Spain.
Last night's fire still smoldering in a pit at his feet,
a deer-bone flute leaning against a limestone wall.
He picks up a chunk of charcoal to warm his hands
but it burns him, so he hurls it against the wall
snarling in surprise, shaking his hand as if the
pain were a spider he could fling away.

Before long, he's staring at the gray streak the charcoal
left on his wall, and he's so hungry he suddenly sees the
profile of a buffalo. He grabs a cold hunk of coal and
blackens the body in, then laughs and adds a spear:
a last minute wish. Then the wall scene happens. In a
nearby field. The buffalo lumbers past. He kills it with a
spear. He feasts beside his fire, staring at the buffalo on his
wall, wagging his head, grunting in amazement.

Stars swim up from the horizon, but the moon out-stars
them all, pregnant in the heavens, bright enough to light
the cave, even when his fire wanes. He grabs a half-charred
stick, approaches the wall, outlines a naked woman
with long, dark hair and swollen breasts.

He gashes his finger with a bone knife for blood to color
her nipples and lips, and stares hopefully at his second
painting, with another hunger: loneliness.
Then he stares expectantly at the forest with his
bleeding hand over his heart.
Our unshaven king of the caverns
has just invented art.

# Undressing a Mango

She opens through a single slit
and the sun pours through her skin.
Her green lips pull back with a touch
so slight, it's almost effortless. And
when you touch your mouth to her body,
you're suddenly speaking another language
whose every adjective is another shade
of sweetness, whose nouns are orange
rooms with orange pillows and orange beds,
whose verbs are all the ways love can be made,
the ways fire masquerades as flesh.
When you close your eyes and
taste her, you see a woman's face. Freckled
with sunlight, daubed with bronze, chiseled by wind.
It doesn't matter if you are a deer or a dog,
a man or a woman. You have swallowed
her secret sugar. You have tugged on
her seed with your teeth. You are hers and she is yours.
You will devour her again and again.
Your hand on the curve of her gravity,
her warm paint dripping from your lips.

# The Tortoise and the Rain

He lives in a brown house. He marches it around.
His hands like shrunken boxing gloves.
His spine a dome of shingles. He doesn't live on
this Earth, he is it. A hard nipple adrift
on our planet's skin. Only, he doesn't drift far. For the
hundredth day he's crunching around in the leaves
beyond the porch, yanking raw dandelions into his
mouth, chewing them without a sound.
The hairline in his cheek seems to smile when his jaw
clamps down. What is he smiling at? Nothing? Everything?
His obsidian eyes lift, unblinking, towards
black thunder, hovering clouds,
which could collapse into waterfalls any moment now.
But our hero, our stoic cowboy in his one gallon shell,
just lowers his face back to the endless salad
on the warm platter of the ground.
Through the paper-thin pane of my window
I watch lightning rip a crooked poem across the sky.
The tortoise doesn't care; that light is his light.
That speed and singe is also a part of him.
But I can't help rushing outside when the storm
begins to pound on the little leather knob of
his head. I wrap my dripping hands around the carved
edges of his shell, lifting him away from the grass,
setting him down in the shelter of the porch.
I return to my seat by the window.
He stretches his neck like a question mark.
One glance left, one glance right.
A wall of rain at each edge of the porch.
He nods his head, flexes his legs,
and marches like God into the downpour.

# The Stone Age

Today, I am probably a rock,
rolling down the asphalt road with
a thousand other rocks, banging
into the garbage cans of things
I no longer want, ricocheting off
telephone poles, with their wires
full of words, above. Chipping my
sharp edges on lightposts, tumbling
through this river of humans,
grinding my rough spots off.

Like a jawbreaker whose layers
get sweeter as the tongue swirls towards
the core, I am tumbling in the ravenous
mouth of the world. I will rub the mud
down to agate, then scrape the agate
down to quartz. A little deeper in, and
I'll glimmer like snowflake obsidian.
Then the feline gold of tiger's eye,
the purple pulse of amethyst. Another
thousand days like this and I'll be
diamond, flawless, spirit.

# Austin Astronaut

Near the overpass
I watch the mahogany hand of a homeless man
receive a bright green apple from
a silver link in the long chain of cars.
So many cars that their brake lights look like lines of
patient, red stars. As he stoops to set the apple down
on the concrete median and begins to steadily walk
away from it, his cardboard sign telling us
he's a veteran, he needs help, God Bless,
I begin to wonder if hunger is a planet,
circling our stunning sun along with the Moons
of Loneliness, the Venus of Lust, and farther and
farther out are planets happy with the least,
small worlds of satisfaction, fullness, satiety.
The homeless man keeps hobbling away,
every step is a lost orbit
and the planet Granny Smith keeps receding
its juice so bittersweet, so distant.

# The Invention of Applause

I always envision them in overalls:
five or six sun-beaten men standing at the edge of a field
of shriveled corn or withered wheat
a field that might belong to any or all of them
just as rain belongs to everyone who prays for it.

Their hands are as cracked as the soil under their heels.
Their eyes are the only wet pools on a thousand dry acres.
But out beyond the prairie grass that separates the crops
the sky is growing darker than any of their hearts,
hearts that have pumped dust for the last four months.

Then, the tallest one spits, an act of pure abundance,
a hundred dollar bill used to light the evening fire.

Their noses flare as if they can smell
the dancer in the distance,
the million-footed beauty whose
very breath brings wet.

As her tiny, clear toes pound the soil,
smudging the dust on their upturned faces
one, then two, then six begin to clap their hands together,
approximating, in their straight-faced way,
the sound a downfall makes.

So that when the storm is over they can close their eyes
and hear salvation again and again
so when the storm has passed they can clap and clap
and still hear the wonder of rain.

# Sitting With The Psychic

You already know the reason
I'm writing this. You've probably read it
in the purple pages of the comic books
that flap through my mind. The superhero
or supervillain (only you know which one I am)
treks up an alpine mountain
through a thousand clapping aspens.

And you probably know his bare feet aren't blistered
when he reaches the snow-crusted rocks.
He sits there, warm in my thoughts,
which you read with a sly little nod,
as if you suddenly heard a can of thunder
being opened in the kitchen of God,
as if you'd known this would happen all along,
he would hike to the top of the world and a tiny blue
bomb would go off in his heart.
Not the kind built by generals,
but the kind lit by a certain woman's smile,
the kind sparked by midnight stars.
Not the kind that kills men suddenly,
but the kind that turns
their lives to art.

# Resolution

In Denmark, the New Year's Eve fun begins
by gathering old dishes and winging them
at the houses of friends.
While Mexicans, too poor to obliterate dishes,
eat twelve grapes and make twelve wishes.
When the clock creeps towards midnight,
these Mexicans, refreshed by their feast
of a dozen grapes, haul their suitcases
around the block so the New Year will
carry them to distant landscapes,
to cities like Chicago where they can stand in the wind
eating popcorn with pigeons.

In Paris, the citizens vomit through
windows onto the sidewalk, a drunken
ritual for releasing the past: this brings
luck to no one except hungry stray
poodles and their cousins, the rats.

To bring New Year's luck in Rio de Janeiro,
the locals flock to a beach called Copacabana,
leap seven waves and drown flowers for the
goddess Yemanja.

The Sicilians, big surprise, eat lasagna.

But here in the Country of Poetry
we wander out under the stars
with champagne glasses filled with ink
with sheets of paper like this one
blooming from our spines like wings.

# Where The Wild Things Hide

It has been almost a decade
since we spoke each other's names.
Since two trees fell in a forest
where no one was listening,
leaving two holes in the ground
where, as it turns out, two
small foxes live now. And
at night, they come out,
wary of owls, their two plumes
of breath moistening the star-lit air.
Sometimes they find each other,
two sets of startled eyes
pretending not to remember
as if forgetting was a choice
while across the world
a famous singer shatters
a turquoise gemstone
with her voice.

# Poem Zoo

They keep the Love poems in tall cages
so they can fold and unfold their wings
dropping letters like feathers
until the floor is caked with meaning.

Academic poems are quarantined
in long halls whose walls are etched
with allusions to the Roman pantheon,
the much-remembered Greeks.
These scrawny poems pace up and down
trying to figure themselves out.

Nature poems swirl across the moat
near the entrance bridge, their sun-baked lines
hard as alligator hide, their eyes
like ancient amber spheres.

The poems of loss are kept in a pit of quicksand.
For five dollars you can buy a stick
and try to rescue them.

Sea poems swim through aquariums
filled with ink. At the tops of the tanks
curl tiny paper waves.

And then there are the poems of night
the poems in which the moon appears,
in which the sun seems to have died:
They hang in a cave so dark all you see
are the stars of their sleepless eyes.

# Methuselah

Today, it seems, I'm turning 217
in dog years, which might feel ancient
if I wasn't sitting here silently in the body of a man.
If, instead, I was a Labrador curled on the floor
or even a Bull Mastiff with my nose
pressed like a racquetball to the window.

If, like an Andes Shaman, I could
shape-shift at will, I might find myself
even older. A ferret pushing five-hundred,
a moon snail creeping up on my first millennium.

In spider-years, I might be so old as to
have witnessed the formation of this continent,
to have watched Europeans ferry the Atlantic.
I could spin a comprehensive history
in this afternoon's web.

In butterfly-years, I would be almost infinite,
with my blue, iridescent wings. Since most
of my fellow caterpillar angels never
last more than two weeks,
that would clock me in at 2,864,513.

Old enough to flap, laughing, past the
Parthenon and Stonehenge, past all those
modern, man-made things.

Even past the newborn pyramids
in the Valley of the Kings.

# Womb Song

A father is reading poems
to his unborn son and wife
as she sits on a velvet, green loveseat
her naked stomach swollen like a zeppelin
ready to rise into the night,
its tiny pilot tired of being a fish, ready for a sky
whose clouds are breasts, whose rains
are warm summer milk.

Her husband's voice is so sincere
so gentle in its picking the tangerines
of meaning and squeezing them in their ears
that she falls asleep, unexpectedly, her lips
kissing open, like a goldfish, while the
swimmer in her womb flutters his fins
and continues to listen.

His father reads on, knowing his son is there,
floating in the darkness, with candle-dim images
flickering all around him, reflections in the puddles of
pulse, in the ocean of his mother's dreams.

In this ocean where he normally swims alone,
tonight there are nets of language
and he climbs them towards his father's voice
towards the day he will be born
towards the year he'll find this poem
age five or six, maybe more
and know how this life was written for him
and know he has lived it before.

# Songs

# If I Was Away

Maybe next winter I'll send you a ring, to wear on your finger,
to help you to sing a song for a man who is too far away
who sits in the distance with nothing to say.

If I was a radio I'd tune this song for you about the things
I might have been in worlds we never knew.
If I was a record I would spin and spin and spin, 'cause time is
just a needle on this skin I'm living in.
If I was some speakers I would roar to outer space.
And if I was awaaaaaay, I'd come back to you someday...

This is the distance between you and me.
How many footsteps more do I need?
How many fires until we find wood?
How many nights don't we sleep when we should?

If I was a river I would flow right through your life and wash
away the darkness like day erases night. If I was a house I would
hold back heavy snow and keep your books and blankets warm
each time you go. If I was a dancer I would cross this open stage.
and if I was awaaaaaay, I'd come back to you someday...

Maybe next summer or I don't know when
I'll drive across Kansas and find you again,
in your yellow dress with those tears still on your face
I'll lift you and kiss you and take you away.

If I was a breath, I would fill your empty chest
with all wind that I could fit inside my fishing net.
If I was a fire, I would burn right through this wind
and let you know the kind of smoke and ash I'm living in.
If I was a poet I would know just what to say.
And if I was awaaaaaay, I'd come back to you someday...

# The House of Alfred King

I saw an old man on his porch a'swinging on his swing.
He said hey young'un set a spell and listen to me sing.
I asked him what the year was, he said nineteen-forty three.
I asked him where his mind was,
he turned and sang to me:

*I'm a little bit weak in the knees. I'm a little bit lonely.*
*I'm a little bit longing for the girl I knew when I was seventeen.*

I asked him if he'd seen the war.
That's where he earned his purple heart.
Back home he left behind a gal.
I asked him where she was now.

He didn't even have a clue, he said his whole life had
turned blue. My heart went right out to that man,
he shed a tear and and sang again:

*I'm a little bit weak in the knees. I'm a little bit lonely...*

When his second verse was done I looked out towards the
setting sun. I saw a woman at the gate.
I knew she hadn't come too late.

Once on the porch, she inquired, "Is this the house
of Alfred King?" I watched his face light up like fire
she looked down and began to sing:

*I'm a little bit weak in the knees. I'm a little bit lonely.*
*I'm a little bit longing for the boy I knew when I was seventeen.*

# Windchimes (Glad Man)

I can hear my neighbor's windchimes they're chimin' in
the night and you won't be here tomorrow though you
were here tonight
*and I'm a sad, sad man, saddest man I ever been.*

I can see you in your nightclothes, I can feel
you next to me. When it's time for you to go
I curl up in the sheets
*and I'm a sad, sad man, saddest man there's ever been.*

I listen to the whippoorwills in the woods outside my
house. I don't want you someday, baby
I want you right now
*and I'm a sad, sad man, saddest man I ever been.*

You'll be back again love when your hard work is done.
Until then I close my eyes I cannot stand the sun
*and I'm a sad, sad man, saddest man there's ever been.*

And though it's only Thursday night I know it won't be
long 'till you're right here with me in this room
'till you're right here in my arms
*and I'm a glad, glad man, gladdest man I ever been.*

I can hear my neighbor's windchimes they're chimin' in
the night and you'll be here tomorrow though you were
not here tonight
*and I'm a glad, glad man, gladdest man there's ever been.*

# Everytime

Everytime I run, everytime I fall.
Everytime the sun paints the western wall.
Everytime I stand before the ocean blue
my feet covered in sand, I think of you.

Everytime the rain paints the bushes black.
Everytime the wind makes the treetops laugh.
Every single thing I win, single thing I lose
when I start to sing, I think of you.

Everytime my face hits the pillowcase.
Everytime the clouds drift in funny shapes.
Everytime the stars gather 'round the moon
no matter where you are, I think of you.

Everytime the night brings the cold around
Everytime I leave this sleepy mountain town
Everywhere I go, everything I do
my boots covered in snow, I think of you.

# Dance You Around

I've been waking up at sunset
singing good morning to the stars
I brush my teeth for Jesus
and set out into the dark.

*And you know that sooner or later*
*I'm gonna take you in my arms*
*and dance you around,*
*dance you around, dance you around*
*until the night comes down.*

School is out for the summer
and the weather's getting warm
so take off your favorite sweater
and come meet me in the barn.

*And you know that sooner or later...*

The crickets are in the bushes
whistling up a storm
The fire's tiny embers
cast shadows of your form.

*And you know that sooner or later...*

Of all the people I pray for
to keep them safe from harm
You're the one that I've made for
this room in my crimson heart.

*And you know that sooner or later...*

# We Won't Wait for the World to Change

I woke up this morning with this song in my hands.
The dreams of my father were turning to glass.
And my beautiful mother was shaking her head.
I threw on my boots and I leapt out of bed.

*We won't wait for the world to change.*
*We won't wait for the sleepers to wake.*
*We'll step out into these streets and be brave.*
*We won't wait for the world to change.*

We're just trying to make some sense of this place.
This concert of colors and summers and shapes.
There's a parrot perched on our shoulder who says
that the earth is collapsing right under our beds.

*We won't wait for the world to change...*

It's not about saving the people and the pets.
There's a deal being made between the living and the
dead. Between the queen of the trees and the ocean's
sweet depth, between earning a buck and taking a breath.

*We won't wait for the world to change...*

They say you can only keep what you give.
We're hungry for something, don't know what it is.
But the blizzard is coming, so give me a kiss
while the moon paints another night on our skin.

*We won't wait for the world to change...*

# Stay

You left for work and I spent the morning with music.
My mom's old guitar and nobody 'round here to use it.
A house isn't made out of bricks, it's made out of beauty.
I can feel my whole life in your arms when you're holding
on to me.

And I know I should go out into the day
and make some contribution to the crazy parade
but I stay, I stay, I staaaayaaayaaaayaay.

This is my life, I live it sometimes like a gypsy.
I wander the streets and paint pictures of things that
amuse me. I sit by the window and let the big sun shine
right through me. Then when you come home, my heart
jumps up just like a puppy.

I'd quit my job and go fishing at night in the rain.
If come Monday morning you'd throw your alarm clock
away and you'd stay, you'd stay, you'd staaaayaaayaaaayaay.

We went out last night and flew kites on the beach and
got dirty. We laughed as the moon crossed the sky, it was
suddenly morning. A life isn't made out of time, it's made
out of beauty. I can feel my whole life in your arms when
you're holding on to me.

You fell asleep next to me at the start of the day.
I watched you drift into dreams with my eyes full of flames
and we stay, we stay, we staaaayaaayaaaayaay.

# Blue Blessings

What can you get from a man with a pen?
A guitar that he's learning to play?
A car with no seats and a bucket of dreams
and a suitcase of sunshine and rain?
*Some men bring you roses, some men bring you bones.*
*I bring you so much love, more than you'll ever know.*

I flew across the big ocean
to a country where nobody goes
You packed up your bags and followed me there
took my hand and I followed you home
*Some men bring you roses, some men bring you gold...*

What can you get from a man with two lips?
Who wakes up in the middle of the day?
Who sits and writes poems as if they were worth more
than just paper and ink, joy and pain?
*Some men bring you roses, some men bring you stones...*

I feel like I've known you forever
not just four months and four weeks
your kisses are wise and courageous
and they fall like blue blessings on me.
*Some men bring you roses, some men bring you snow...*

What can you get from a man with big wings?
That nobody but you can see?
He's an angel sometimes and a devil by night
and he burns like the world's never seen.
*Some men bring you roses, some men bring you coal...*

# Hurricane

Fifteen centuries ago, they never knew just when
she would blast into the coast and lash them all with wind.
They would all start running in the drums of sudden rain.
Now we know she's coming and we even know her name.

Hurri-hurri-hurri-hurri-cane. Teach us how to help each
other, teach us how to pray. Teach us how to hold on while
our lives get swept away. When everything we know gets
broken by the winds of change.

The Ocean, she gets hotter almost every single day.
She's running a bad fever and it looks like we're to blame
the ones who pump the chemicals into our waterways
the ones who pass the laws that make our planet pay.

Hurri-hurri-hurri-hurri-cane. When you gonna come and
blow this crooked country straight? Teach us how to fix
the wind, how to heal the rain. Teach us how to clean the
things that greed has made us stain.

We put up steel shutters and we fill our water jugs.
We listen to the radio and wait for you to come.
We've got a dozen candles and a little book of flame.
We'll keep the floodlights burning 'till the power fades
away.

Hurri-hurri-hurri-hurri-cane. Forgive the things we've done
as we learned to find our way. Teach us how to help this
planet, teach us how to pray. Teach us how to hunker
down, teach us how to stay.

# Put me in a Box with your Mom

Had lunch with my daddy the other day
his jeans were all muddy and splattered with paint.
He was fixing up the house while Mom was away.
He said your mom and I should settle down some day
but the way we work and the way we play
our only rest might be in the cold, dark grave.
So when our final, fiery sunset comes
put me in a box with your mom.

*Put me in a box with your mom
then forever I can hold her in my arms.
When all our days on earth are spent and gone
put me in a box with your mom.*

We met in high school in sixty-eight
ate burgers and French fries on our first date.
Her daddy said better not keep her out late
but I kept her so long she's still with me today.
In a churchhouse on the Pennsylvania line
I became her husband, she became my wife:
'till death do us part and beyond
*put me in a box with your mom...*

Folks don't stay together nowadays. They fight and they
fly and they run away. Even though our skies sometimes
looked gray, your mom stuck with me all the way.
Raising two wild babies, we were brave.
The scent of diapers mixed with aftershave.
now our little ones are grown and gone
and I'm happy in this house with your mom.
*Put me in a box with your mom...*

# Heavyweight Champion of the Night

Remember this chest. Remember this breath. Remember this
weight. It's all that I have. Remember these hands in the small
of your back. Remember the way that my songs made you laugh.
This is the weight of passenger trains. This is the weight of all I
can't say. This is the weight of my fists as they're lifted to fight
anytime anyone anywhere might make you cry. *I am the
Heavyweight Champion. I am the Heavyweight Champion.
I am the Heavyweight Champion of the Night.*

Remember these arms. Remember these legs. Remember the
sea on the raft of our bed. Remember my purple, my pink and
my red. Remember I slept with my hand on your head. This
is the weight of when I went away. This is the weight of those
telephone wires. This is the weight of my fists as they're lifted to
fight anytime anyone anywhere might make you cry.
*I am the Heavyweight Champion...*

Remember the rooms I lived in with you. Remember the songs
I pulled from your womb. Remember the summer of wonderful
rain. Remember again and again and again. This is the weight of
my lips on your lips. This is the weight of my ribs on your ribs.
This is the weight of my wings as they're lifted to fly
you anywhere anytime, any night.
*I am the Heavyweight Champion...*

Remember these hands. Remember these knees. Remember
the night we flew kites by the sea. Remember the strange and
remarkable tastes.  Remember the blindfold I tied on your face.
This is the weight of two small, pale objects dropped from a
tower, from Newton's fists, falling at the same sweet speed
in the gravity of happiness, in the gravity of happiness,
in the happiness of gravity.
*I am the Heavyweight Champion...*

# Wildcats

We woke up so early again, flipped out of bed like cat-fish
into our shirts and blue-jeans, we flew out the door with
nothing to eat.
*Life keeps movin' too fast, keeps a runnin' away like wildcats*
*into the woods where wise old fools would say:*
*you never took the time to live your life anyway*
*What can you say? Heeeey! Heeeeeey!*

There always are nine things to do and ten left from
yesterday staring at you. You wish you could wipe the
slate clean, wipe out the math and the history.
*Life keeps movin' too fast, keeps a runnin' away like wildcats*
*onto a stage where the curtains pull away*
*so make sure you're not an actor in someone else's play.*
*Then what would you say? Heeeey! Heeeeeey!*

You hit the bed hard as a stone. A quick kiss goodnight
and you're gone. You grab as much sleep as you can
'cause tomorrow it all starts over again.
*Life keeps movin' too fast, keeps a runnin' away like wildcats*
*into a field where the wind and the daffodils play.*
*Now's the time to live your life your way.*
*What do you say? Heeeey! Heeeeeey!*
*Life keeps movin' too fast, keeps a runnin' away like wildcats...*

*When all you really want to do is stay*
*Why don't you stay? Heeeey! Heeeeeey!*
*Life keeps movin' too fast, keeps a runnin' away like wildcats...*

# The Front Porch of Your Life

You want to know how I'm feeling tonight? I'm fine.
You want to know all the places we'll go when you become
my wife.

It's Ok to go slowly when night falls. It's alright to stay up
all night when your lover comes to call. I'll throw you a
rope and then we can go and nobody has to fall.
*I'm the light on the front porch of your life.*
*You are the sigh when the priest says kiss the bride.*
*How many miles over the mountain side?*
*How many breaths, how many steps, how many goodbyes?*

I wonder where we'll wander when we're old enough to fly
when we've learned our lessons, packed our possessions,
given up on pride. When all we need for freedom is the
blue sky in our eyes.
*I'm the light on the front porch of your life.*
*You are the sigh when the priest says kiss the bride.*
*How many miles over the mountain side?*
*How many breaths, how many steps, how many oceans wide?*

It's Ok to go slowly when night falls.
It's alright to leave a letter on your Daddy's desk at dawn.
I'll build you a bridge and we can go live on an island
without time.
*I'm the light on the front porch of your life.*
*You are the sigh when the priest says kiss the bride.*
*How many miles over the mountain side? How many breaths,*
*how many steps, how many bright fires?*

# Happy

It's been three hundred sixty-five nights since the time we first
kissed and I can't stand a day without tasting your beautiful lips.
I wish I could tell you, how much I adore you, just how much
I love and how deep. But there's no way to say it, no words to
contain it, no poem, no song, no sea.
The best I can do is to call down the moon and ask her to tell
you for me, that you are the sun that shines behind my eyes and
lights up a world of dark streets.
*O Happy, I'm so happy, so happy I can barely sing.*
*Happy, O, so happy, happy, Happy Anniversary.*

When we go to sleep I still want  to just hold you and talk
'till the sun splits the blinds with the light of another bright
dawn. The night that I met you, the sun never set you walked in
with your black guitar and I wanted to take you right home with
me, home to my heart.
But the best I could do was to call down the moon and ask her
to tell you so sweet that you are the one that I was waiting on
the girl this whole world made for me.
*O Happy, I'm so happy, so happy I can barely sing...*

You played your music for winners and losers and most of us
caught in between the stars overhead and the dark riverbeds,
the sad nets so few of us see. Some of them laughed and some
of them clapped and I sat in the back like a king, so rich with
the sounds from your wonderful mouth
so rich from the listening.

And when you were through, I called down the moon and asked
her to take us away to some place in the trees, not so far from
the sea where I could love you the rest of my days.
*O Happy, I'm so happy, so happy I can barely sing.*
*Happy, O, so happy, happy, Happy Anniversary.*

# The Sun is Going Down in Nashville

It's been seven years since the night you just packed up and
went. We both said goodbye not goodnight and we haven't
spoke since. I still find the time to think about you now and
again. I wrote you this song and sang it straight into the wind.
*The sun is going down without you but I can still recall your pretty*
*voice. The sun is going down in Nashville*
*and I'd be with you if I had a choice.*
*Heeeey, Heeeey, Likeariveritslipsaway, Likeariveritslipsaway...*

We dumped the canoe in the river and we lost our keys.
We drowned the camera with pictures of you and of me.
We stood on the banks of that river so naked and free.
You taught me the words to a song that I just couldn't sing.
*The sun is going down without you but I can still recall your pretty*
*smile. The sun is going down in Nashville*
*and I wish you were with me for a while.*
*Heeeey, Heeeey, Likeariveritslipsaway, Likeariveritslipsaway...*

I remember the way you laughed and tried everything twice.
And I dried the tears that the radio brought to your eyes.
I remember the travels that made you so sad and so wise.
I remember the man who built wings and fell out of the sky.
*The sun is going down without you and I wish I could hold your pretty*
*hand. The sun is going down in Nashville and I wish I was still your*
*loving man. Heeeey, Heeeey...Likeariveritslipsaway...*

So long ago, those cold nights when we slept like orphans
wrapped in the blue cocoons of your grandmother's quilts.
Then the world slipped in, slipped in for the kill.
I haven't seen you since and I never will.
*The sun is going down without you and I wish you had been my winter*
*wife. The sun is going down in Nashville. Girl I would have loved you*
*all my life. Heeeey, Heeeey...Likeariveritslipsaway...*

# You & I

When I look in your eyes I watch the carousel ride.
Blue horses are spinnin' with all of the children
who want to fly.

*You say you want to change the world.*
*You couldn't stop it changing if you tried.*
*Everything's changing day after day*
*except you and I.*

*That's a life I want to live. A life I want to try.*
*Everything changing day after day except you and I.*

We meet in the trees of the night
and kiss as if setting a fire.
Somehow I know, wherever we go we'll be burning bright.

*You say you want to change the world...*

So let that old carousel spin as tigers and unicorns sigh.
Forgiveness is wind on all of the things
that we've left behind.

*You say you want to change the world...*

There's an ocean we have to swim
like swans in the waters of time
but somehow I'm sure when we reach the shore
you'll be by my side.

*You say you want to change the world...*

# The Orphan Trains

A thousand ragged orphans board a train on Saturday.
The sun is out there somewhere though the sky is damp
and gray.
Little Alfred sits with his small cardboard suitcase,
his face pressed to the window New York City falls away.

*The Orphan Trains roll west through the rain*
*and no one knows these kids are coming, no one knows their*
*names. And all the orphans sit beside their windows, cry and say:*
*Who would ever really want to love me anyway?*
*Who would ever really want to love me anyway?*
*The Orphan Trains, The Orphan Trains, The Orphan Trains,*
*The Orphan Trains.*

All the children line up on a broken plywood stage.
Their faces have been washed and their clothes are clean
and straight. A farmer fingers Emma's teeth just like he
would a mule, but Emma kicks him, screaming, "I'm not
going home with you!"

*The Orphan Trains roll west through the rain...*

Emma is adopted, grows up laughing by a pond.
Into Texas into Kansas the train moves Alfred along.
When they reach Nebraska a town merchant takes him in
sits him on his knee and says, "From now on
you're my kin."

*The Orphan Trains roll west through the rain...*

# Ride Samurai Ride

He spent a long summer with sun and with thunder out on the edge of the world where tigers creep down from the snow covered mountains and carry away little girls. He didn't know what had happened back home, a new clan had conquered the town and the prince that he lived to defend was now sleeping in a dark hole in the ground.

*Ride Samurai Ride! The fortress has fallen with your*
*children inside. This is the reason you kept your sword sharpened,*
*tomorrow you'll live or you'll die. So, Ride Samurai Ride, Ride Samurai*
*Ride...*

You killed your first villain when you were just ten. A thief came to kidnap the prince. He was asleep in a cradle of dragons. The blood splattered freckles on him. And now he's gone, they killed him unarmed, it had to happen someday. But why at a time when you couldn't defend him, when you were so far away?

*Ride Samurai Ride! They've killed your father, they've captured your*
*wife. This is the reason you kept your sword sharpened, tomorrow you'll*
*live and they'll die.*
*So, Ride Samurai Ride, Ride Samurai Ride...*

When you arrive there are five hundred soldiers so you swing your sword and you kill. You find your wife and your sons and you run to hide them safe in the hills. When you go back for your second attack, you kill the clan's chief in the night. You dig up the body of your brother the prince and sob with the stars in your eyes.

*Ride Samurai Ride! You've reclaimed your fortress, you've reclaimed*
*your life but all that you've lost will never stop haunting the beautiful*
*calm of your mind. So, Ride Samurai Ride...*

# Joan of Arc

The first time I saw her she was up on her horse, her hair in a braid and her eyes on the lord. When I told my father I was off to the war, he gave me a feather as I stepped out the door.

I didn't care too much for God but I fell in love with Joan of Arc. That's why I fought and died for her 'cause I fell in love with Joan of Arc.

We killed and roasted a beautiful fawn, but she wouldn't eat it she sat all alone. I think she was singing I might have been wrong. The wind in my helmet sounded like song.
I didn't care too much for God but I fell in love with Joan...

My heart was a candle and it burned for her then as a cannon shot lifted me into the wind. I was a ghost before I hit the ground but I saw her eyes blinking and two tears rolling down.
I didn't care too much for God but I fell in love with Joan...

JOAN: *I went to fight at the age of nineteen. When the church burned me, I still couldn't read. They promised me mercy, but they wrapped me in flames. Five hundred years later they made me a saint.*

*I didn't care too much for war but I knew I loved him, that I am sure and that's why I fought that's why I fought and died for God 'cause he kept his promise to teach me to love.*

*I didn't know my lonely Knight's name when they cast my ashes into the Seine. But I saw his face, yes, I saw his face as the church turned my body to ashes again.*

As God turned her beauty to ashes again.
I didn't care too much for God but I fell in love with Joan...

# If You Take Then I Will Give

If I walked across the sea would you walk along with me
our footsteps on the tides and waves upon our thighs?

*I just want to grab you in my arms.*
*I want to breathe you in my lungs*
*and set continents adrift.*
*If you take then I will give. If you take then I will give.*

There are stations of the cross where blood no longer falls
and people board their trains as if leaving left no stain.

*I just want to roll into the night*
*I want to hold you in my eyes*
*In this bedroom where we live*
*If you take then I will give. If you take then I will give.*

There are storms when you are sad and sunshine
when you laugh. If you don't know which way to go
just reach out for my hand.

*I just want to shake the day away. I want touch your*
*blushing face. In this small house where we live.*
*If you take then I will give. If you take then I will give.*

There are countries in your soul where men have never
roamed. If I turned my hands to light
would you let me inside?

*I just want to sail into the west, on a ship made out of breath*
*with the wind of your bright kiss.*
*If you take then I will give. If you take then I will give.*

# Lauren's Forest

We went down to Lauren's Forest just the other afternoon.
She was buried in those cedars seven years ago last June.
I can't remember how she smiled, I dug a hundred
pictures out and threw them all into the fire and nearly
burned our new house down.

*Breathing in, I'm breathing in. Breathing out, I'm breathing out.*
*Feel the sunlight on my skin feel my feet upon the ground.*
*Now, oooooooh Now. Now, oooooooh Now.*

Just three weeks before our wedding she went swimming in
the lake. I found her body pale and floating like a boat in
outer space. I couldn't stop my eyes from crying, my voice
from calling her name out. On the day we planned our
wedding, I put my shotgun in my mouth.

*Breathing in, I'm breathing in. Breathing out...*

I was sitting in the closet when her sister Clara came and
reached into my deepest darkness and pulled the shotgun
from my face. I didn't mean to hold her so close, I didn't
mean to touch her skin, but ever since she saved my life,
Clara's been my one true friend.

*Breathing in, I'm breathing in. Breathing out...*

Some nights I hear Lauren whisper: will you come to see
me soon? I know you married my younger sister. I love you
both, you know I do. On a cold and foggy morning,
Clara gave birth to a girl, and now you have a little angel
to carry your name around the world.

# Belize

I flew to New York City just to rent a proper tux.
I remember on the runway how the wind tasted like us.
By that I mean so free and clean our unkissed lips so clear
that even time and his nine thieves saw nothing they could
steal.

*Sometimes I wonder, why did we leave Belize?*
*With you in my arms I had all that a man ever needs.*
*But we left it behind with our eyes on the bright*
*castles of immigrants' dreams.*
*Sometimes I wonder, why did we leave Belize?*

I still keep a picture of the night we went to dance.
We drove to the city in my uncle's rusty van. The orchid
pinned above your heart was just a jungle gift. My mother
sewed some cotton gauze around the humble stem.
*Sometimes I wonder, why did we leave Belize?*

There are symphonies of sentiments I just can't seem to
write. Twenty years of books have covered up that perfect
night. Now you've gone to Boston left our dusty roads
behind. I've heard that you're a doctor that you help fix
people's minds.
*Sometimes I wonder, why did we leave Belize?*

Butterfly, I miss you I will miss you all my life.
If I had the chance for one more dance, I'd make you my
wife. The wind is cold as river stones, the winter's on his
way. But I'll stay warm forever just remembering your face.
*Sometimes I wonder, why did we leave Belize?*

# On the Night You Were Born

Your father ran out through the hospital doors and he
started to shout, "I've got me a boy!" Your mother lay
vanquished and smiling and sore. You were too young to
thank her on the night you were born.

Through night blooming cactus your grandmother came
and said that the angels put your soul in a frame.
And while logs in the fire crackled and roared
the world thought of lions on the night you were born.

Deep in the ocean, two whales sang a song
some say that you heard them, that you hummed along
you opened your eyes and you stared at the door but you
were tired of swimming on the night you were born.

Your grandpa in Georgia saddled his horse
and rode down to Valdosta where whiskey was poured.
Snow fell like secrets that had never been told
and you learned to keep them on the night you were born.

The windows were open in your nursery.
the treefrogs were singing while you fell asleep.
The people were sleeping but the animals roamed and you
dreamt you were with them on the night you were born.

Your parents went down to the lake late that night.
The water was silver, the wind was alive.
It lifted their voices and turned them to song
and the stars were all smiling
on the night you were born.

# Valentine of My Life

I'm the breath that you left on the stage when you sang.
I'm the words like sleeping birds no wind can steal away.
Sometimes poems are made of bones & men are made of
tin. Sometimes valentines arrive in envelopes of skin.

*Ask you again, will I ask you again?*
*I will ask you until I can't speak.*
*If Love is a road that two souls walk upon*
*would you walk that road with me?*
*O Valentine, Valentine, Valentine of my life.*

I'm the lion in the Vatican that only song can tame.
I'm the chandelier of lonely stars beyond the reach of rain.
Sometimes wild worlds reside inside a quiet pen.
Sometimes valentines arrive in envelopes of skin.
*Ask you again, will I ask you again...*

I'm the echo in the mountain's mouth, remembering the
train. I'm the drying child finding out that water leaves no
stain. Sometimes people die not knowing they'll be born
again. Sometimes valentines arrive in envelopes of skin
*Ask you again, will I ask you again...*

I'm the silent little island that no ocean can displace.
I'm the river in December where children go to skate.
Sometimes I just sit and sigh, sometimes I sit and sing.
Sometimes valentines arrive in envelopes of skin.
*Ask you again, will I ask you again...*

*O Valentine, Valentine, Valentine of my life.*

# Bethlehem

The baby Jesus fell asleep beside a newborn lamb. When they
woke up the blood and love and stars were everywhere. Three
young women stood nearby, their breasts swollen with milk,
waiting to give the orphans something beautiful to drink.

*Bethlehem. O, Bethlehem. Just you and I and the big night against our*
*newborn skin. Bethlehem, O, Bethlehem.*
*Sometimes I just walk away I don't know what to sing.*
*O, Bethlehem. O, Bethlehem.*

My handsome father bought a sawed-off shotgun yesterday
and went to hunt his cancer like a fox out in the rain.
He shot it dead and took it's ragged body to the church
and asked the Lord's forgiveness for undoing his dark work.
*Bethlehem. O, Bethlehem...*
*Sometimes I get quiet cause there's nothing left to sing...*

And every one of us a walking drum.
And every one of us knows how to cry and run.
And every one of us comes home sometime.
And every one of us becomes a ghost by and by.

The hurricanes blow in from somewhere we don't understand.
The little orphan learns guitar because no one thinks he can.
He sits out on the broken bridge and strums his humble strings.
He sings about the days to come when strangers take him in.
*Bethlehem. O, Bethlehem...*

I saw the baby Jesus in a seashell on the sand. He was telling
stories to an ancient, naked clam. I leaned in close so I could
know exactly what he said and heard the sound of ocean waves
crashing in his head.
*Bethlehem. O, Bethlehem...*

# ABOUT THE ARTIST

Wolff Bowden grew up in a house on stilts in a swamp near Chuluota, Florida, swimming with alligators, dancing with dragonflies, absorbing the art of the wild.

When his childhood home burned in 1997, Wolff developed a heavily-textured style of polymeric painting to re-create the swamp on canvas. After earning a degree in Natural Science at New College, Wolff was named ARTEXPO ARTIST OF THE MILLENNIUM. This honor launched him into the world of visual art, allowing him to buy time for writing poems through the sale of his paintings. Wolff's artwork hangs in hundreds of private collections. As of this publication, Wolff has been painting for 14 years. To learn more, please visit:

WOLFFANTASTIC.COM

On ferocious winter nights, beside a fire, Wolff sculpts a line of meditative, environmental jewelry in fine silver.
GRATITREE.COM

In the world of Music, Wolff performs as THE MASKED FANTASTIC, writing songs, playing guitar and singing with Dakota Rose in the band THE ORPHAN TRAINS.

THEORPHANTRAINS.COM

Wolff would like to thank his family, friends and collectors for supporting his creative adventures. And he would like to thank the Valentine of His Life for being an unceasing inspiration.